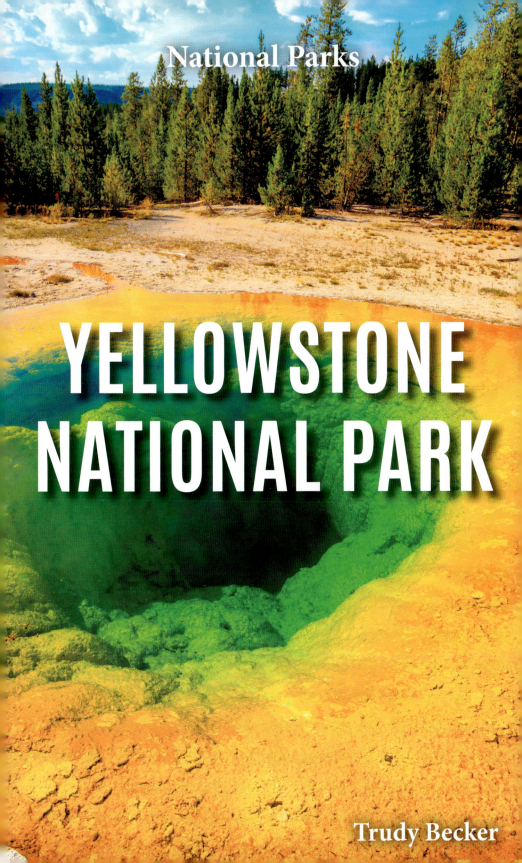

WWW.APEXEDITIONS.COM

Copyright © 2025 by Apex Editions, Mendota Heights, MN 55120. All rights reserved. No part of this book may be reproduced or utilized in any form or by any means without written permission from the publisher.

Apex is distributed by North Star Editions:
sales@northstareditions.com | 888-417-0195

Produced for Apex by Red Line Editorial.

Photographs ©: Shutterstock Images, cover, 1, 6–7, 8–9, 12–13, 14–15, 16–17, 18–19, 30–31, 32–33, 39, 42–43, 44–45, 48–49, 54–55; iStockphoto, 4–5, 10–11, 29, 36–37, 40–41, 46–47, 52–53; National Park Service, 20–21, 58–59; Library of Congress, 22–23, 24–25; Frances Benjamin Johnston/National Park Service, 26–27; Jim Peaco/National Park Service, 34–35; Mike Lewelling/National Park Service, 50–51; Neal Herbert/National Park Service, 56–57; Red Line Editorial, 59

Library of Congress Control Number: 2024943063

ISBN
979-8-89250-456-0 (hardcover)
979-8-89250-472-0 (paperback)
979-8-89250-503-1 (ebook pdf)
979-8-89250-488-1 (hosted ebook)

Printed in the United States of America
Mankato, MN
012025

NOTE TO PARENTS AND EDUCATORS

Apex books are designed to build literacy skills in striving readers. Exciting, high-interest content attracts and holds readers' attention. The text is carefully leveled to allow students to achieve success quickly.

TABLE OF CONTENTS

Chapter 1

SPRAYING WATER 4

Chapter 2

ALL ABOUT YELLOWSTONE 8

Chapter 3

PEOPLE AND YELLOWSTONE 18

Natural Wonder

GRAND PRISMATIC SPRING 28

Chapter 4

FUN AT YELLOWSTONE 31

Natural Wonder

THE GRAND CANYON OF THE YELLOWSTONE 38

Chapter 5

WILDLIFE 40

Chapter 6

SAVING YELLOWSTONE 50

PARK MAP • 58
COMPREHENSION QUESTIONS • 60
GLOSSARY • 62
TO LEARN MORE • 63
ABOUT THE AUTHOR • 63
INDEX • 64

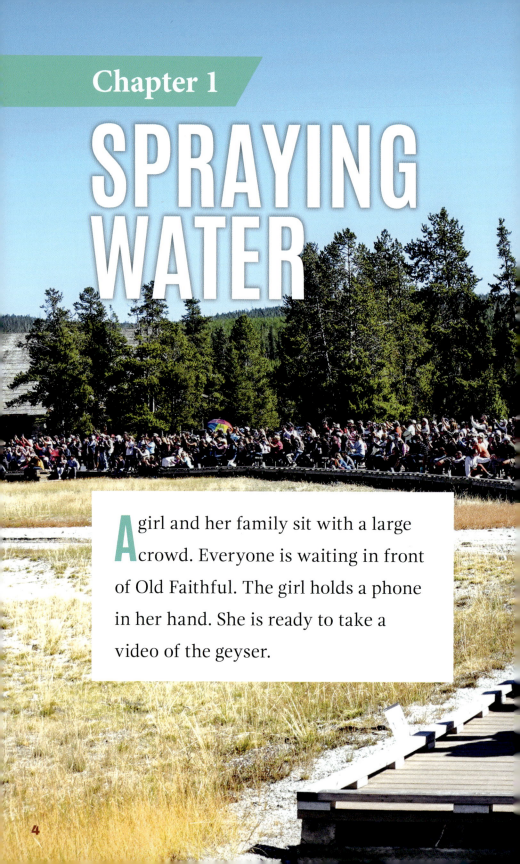

Chapter 1
SPRAYING WATER

A girl and her family sit with a large crowd. Everyone is waiting in front of Old Faithful. The girl holds a phone in her hand. She is ready to take a video of the geyser.

On summer days, about 2,000 people gather to watch each eruption of Old Faithful.

The geyser spouts a small bit of water. It stops quickly. But the girl keeps watching. She knows more is coming. A few minutes later, it happens. Water erupts from the ground. It shoots more than 100 feet (30 m) into the air. The girl takes her video. She smiles at the amazing sight.

LISTENING TO OLD FAITHFUL

When Old Faithful erupts, it roars. The rumbling comes from the land vibrating. However, that isn't the only sound. Eruptions cause people to make noise, too. Visitors often gasp and clap.

Old Faithful's eruption can last up to five minutes.

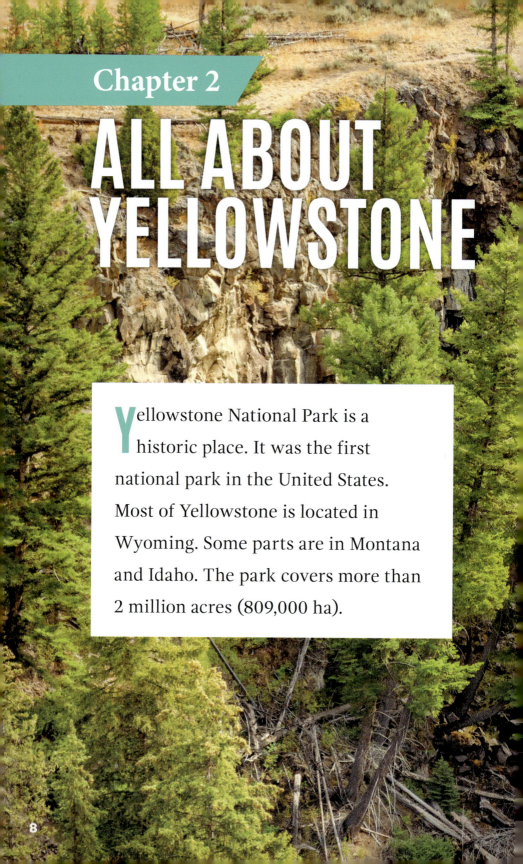

Chapter 2
ALL ABOUT YELLOWSTONE

Yellowstone National Park is a historic place. It was the first national park in the United States. Most of Yellowstone is located in Wyoming. Some parts are in Montana and Idaho. The park covers more than 2 million acres (809,000 ha).

Yellowstone National Park is home to nearly 300 waterfalls.

At Yellowstone's hydrothermal features, steam escapes from deep inside the planet.

The park is on top of a dormant volcano. It is called the Volcanic Caldera. It is also known as the Yellowstone Supervolcano. Below Earth's surface, the supervolcano is very hot. This heat has affected the land in many ways. For example, it created hydrothermal features. Half of the world's hydrothermal features are in Yellowstone.

FORMING THE LAND

Earth's surface sits on huge plates. These plates slowly move and shift. Over millions of years, this movement creates mountains and volcanoes. Plate movements can also send magma to new places. At Yellowstone, hot material has moved close to the surface.

Yellowstone has several types of hydrothermal features. Hot springs are one kind. In these spots, hot water escapes from below the surface. Geysers are similar. Geysers spray water from time to time. Yellowstone has more than 500 geysers. Mud pots are another type. Mud pots look like pools of bubbling mud.

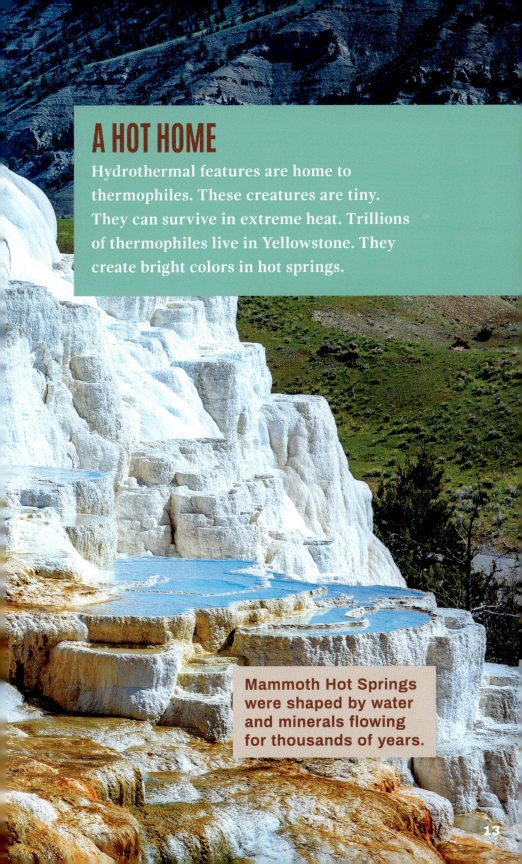

A HOT HOME

Hydrothermal features are home to thermophiles. These creatures are tiny. They can survive in extreme heat. Trillions of thermophiles live in Yellowstone. They create bright colors in hot springs.

Mammoth Hot Springs were shaped by water and minerals flowing for thousands of years.

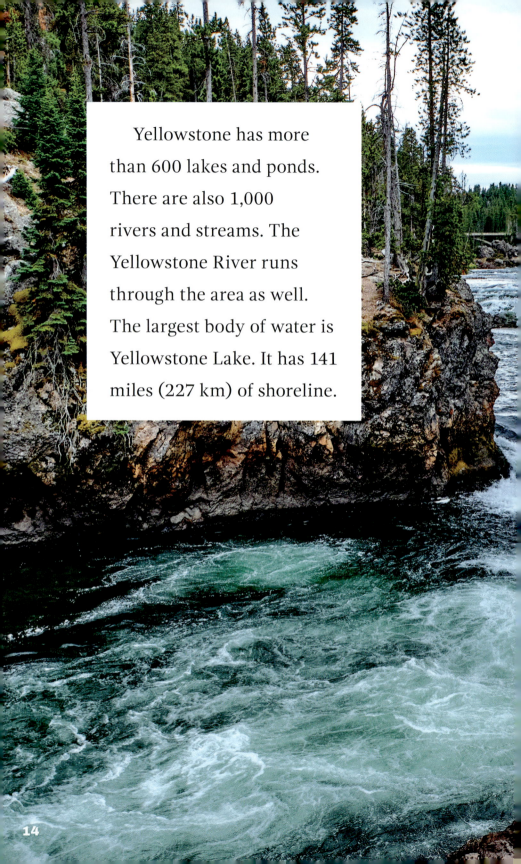

Yellowstone has more than 600 lakes and ponds. There are also 1,000 rivers and streams. The Yellowstone River runs through the area as well. The largest body of water is Yellowstone Lake. It has 141 miles (227 km) of shoreline.

The Madison River flows through Yellowstone for 19 miles (31 km).

BELOW THE SURFACE

The land under Yellowstone Lake is hot. The lake has many vents at the bottom. In some spots, the water can reach 252 degrees Fahrenheit (122°C). Many animals live in the lake. These include worms and sponges.

Yellowstone has many examples of petrified wood. It is one of the largest collections in the world.

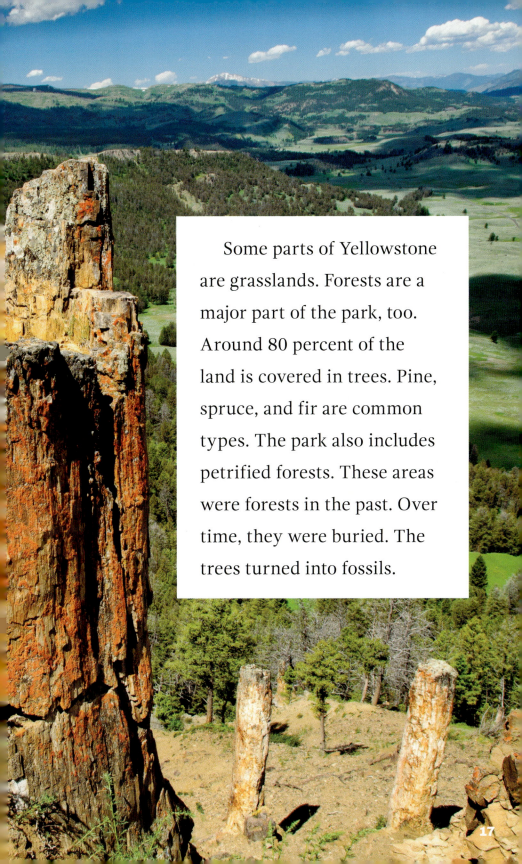

Some parts of Yellowstone are grasslands. Forests are a major part of the park, too. Around 80 percent of the land is covered in trees. Pine, spruce, and fir are common types. The park also includes petrified forests. These areas were forests in the past. Over time, they were buried. The trees turned into fossils.

Chapter 3

PEOPLE AND YELLOWSTONE

Humans have lived near Yellowstone for more than 11,000 years. Many Indigenous peoples have made their homes in the area. The Shoshone and Kiowa people lived in and around Yellowstone. So did the Sioux and Crow people. Bison were an important food source for these groups.

Many Indigenous peoples consider bison to be sacred.

The Tukudika are part of the Shoshone people. They have lived near Yellowstone for thousands of years. In 1835, the Tukudika met white explorers for the first time. Soon, more white people came to the area. They wanted fur and gold. Others came to map the land.

SHEEP EATERS

The Tukudika people hunted bighorn sheep. The name *Tukudika* means "sheep eaters." Nearby Indigenous groups had similar names based on their diets. Some were known as salmon eaters. Others were elk eaters. Today, Tukudika people still live close to Yellowstone.

A group of Shoshone people gather near their tepees in the 1870s.

White settlers took over Indigenous land. They pushed Native people out. In 1871, explorer Ferdinand Hayden studied the area. An artist was part of his crew. The artist painted scenes of the land. Because of this work, more white people learned about the area.

Thomas Moran was one of the first people to paint Yellowstone. He showed his art to Congress.

President Theodore Roosevelt (top left) visited Yellowstone in 1903.

Some white settlers wanted to make their homes on the land. But other people wanted to keep the area wild. Explorers, businesspeople, and lawmakers joined this movement. The project caught on. And in 1872, it succeeded. Yellowstone became the first national park.

MORE PROTECTION

In 1894, the US government passed the Lacy Act. This law protected Yellowstone in more ways. For example, some parts of the law related to animals. It said hunters could not kill and sell bison.

In the late 1800s and early 1900s, the US Army kept Indigenous people from entering Yellowstone.

Creating the first national park was not easy. Government workers had to draw the park's borders. They had to raise money. Also, the area needed roads and buildings for tourists.

For a while, the army worked on Yellowstone. Later, the government created the National Park Service. This group developed the park. By the 2020s, more than three million people visited Yellowstone each year.

Natural Wonder

GRAND PRISMATIC SPRING

Yellowstone's largest hot spring is Grand Prismatic Spring. This spring is 370 feet (113 m) across. That's longer than a football field. And it is more than 120 feet (37 m) deep. That is taller than a 10-story building.

The spring shows off a rainbow of colors. The middle looks blue. This is caused by light hitting the spring. It also has rings of color. They include orange, yellow, and green. The water in these spots varies in temperature.

The water in Grand Prismatic Spring can reach up to 188 degrees Fahrenheit (87°C).

Yellowstone is home to more than 10,000 hydrothermal features.

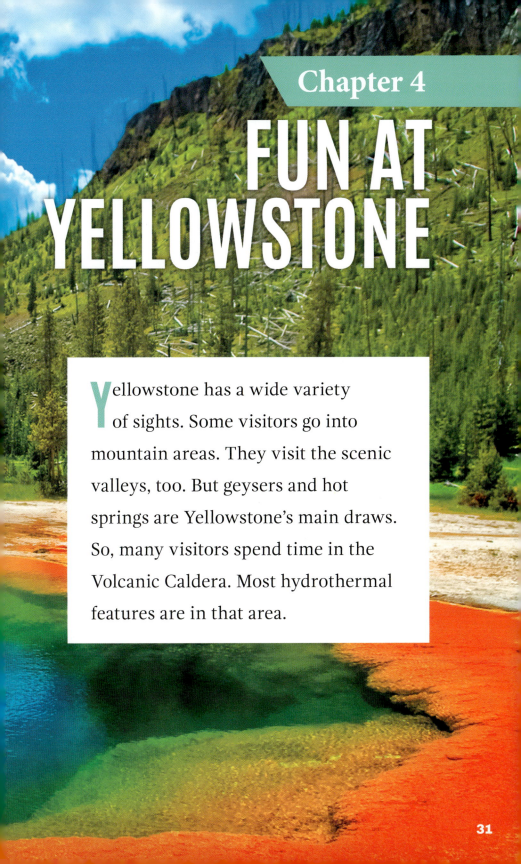

Chapter 4
FUN AT YELLOWSTONE

Yellowstone has a wide variety of sights. Some visitors go into mountain areas. They visit the scenic valleys, too. But geysers and hot springs are Yellowstone's main draws. So, many visitors spend time in the Volcanic Caldera. Most hydrothermal features are in that area.

Old Faithful is the most famous geyser in Yellowstone National Park. It is located in the Upper Geyser Basin area. Its eruptions can reach 180 feet (55 m) into the air. Since 1872, it has erupted more than one million times.

FAITHFUL GEYSER

Old Faithful's name comes from its predictable eruptions. Visitors can trust it to burst often. The rate has slowed over time. But it still erupts several times per day. It usually happens once every two hours.

The rate of Old Faithful's eruptions can be affected by earthquakes and climate.

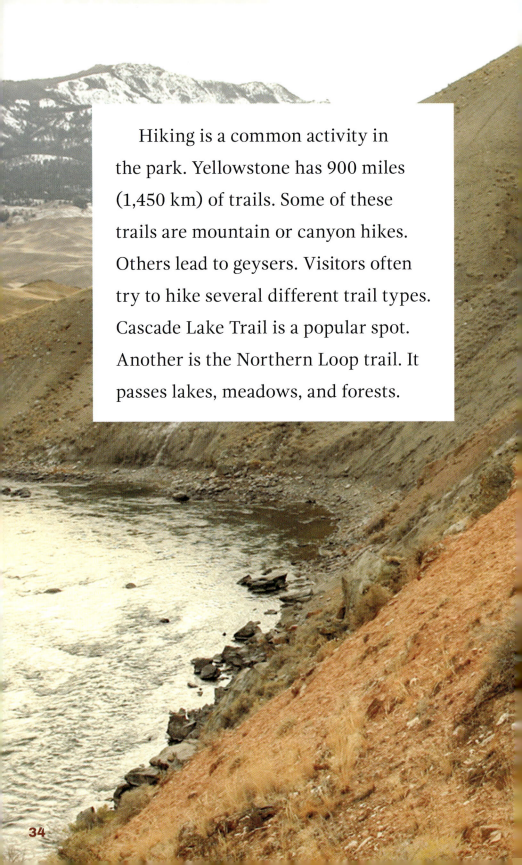

Hiking is a common activity in the park. Yellowstone has 900 miles (1,450 km) of trails. Some of these trails are mountain or canyon hikes. Others lead to geysers. Visitors often try to hike several different trail types. Cascade Lake Trail is a popular spot. Another is the Northern Loop trail. It passes lakes, meadows, and forests.

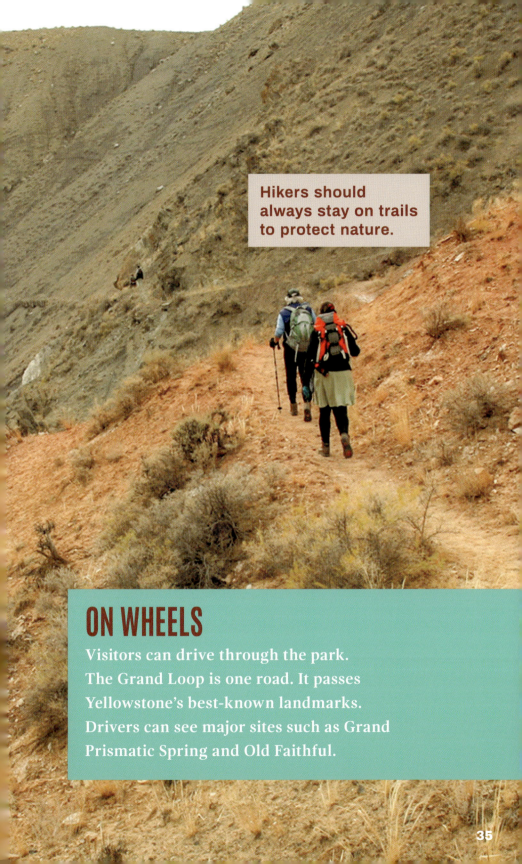

Hikers should always stay on trails to protect nature.

ON WHEELS

Visitors can drive through the park. The Grand Loop is one road. It passes Yellowstone's best-known landmarks. Drivers can see major sites such as Grand Prismatic Spring and Old Faithful.

Some people record the types of fish they catch. This information helps park scientists.

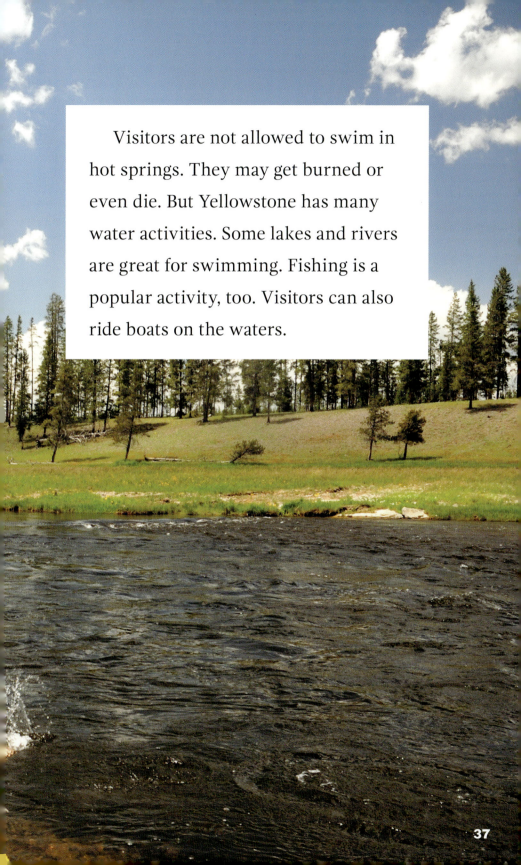

Visitors are not allowed to swim in hot springs. They may get burned or even die. But Yellowstone has many water activities. Some lakes and rivers are great for swimming. Fishing is a popular activity, too. Visitors can also ride boats on the waters.

Natural Wonder

THE GRAND CANYON OF THE YELLOWSTONE

Yellowstone contains a massive canyon. The Yellowstone River carved it over many years. The flowing water eroded the rock. The canyon stretches 17 miles (27 km). Some parts are 4,000 feet (1,200 m) across. And it reaches 1,150 feet (350 m) deep.

People come to see the incredible views. There are several overlooks. Visitors peer down at Yellowstone Falls. They can spot steam rising from the canyon's walls.

The Grand Canyon of the Yellowstone has three waterfalls.

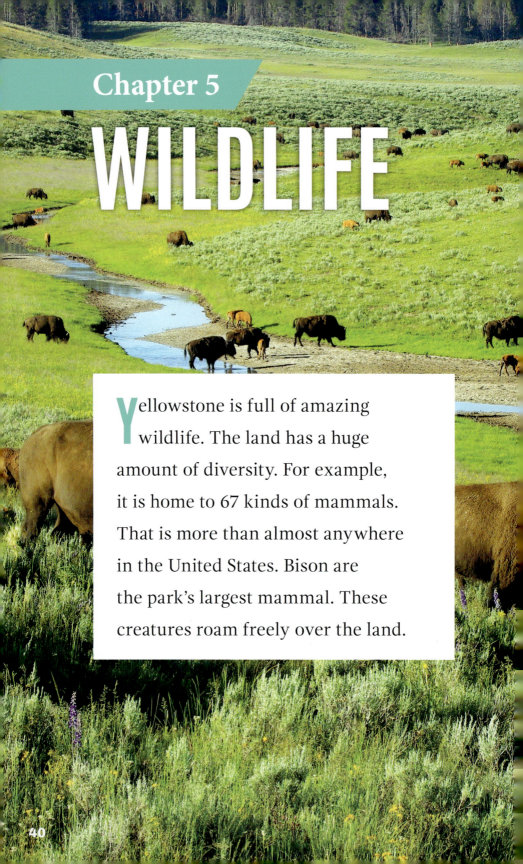

Chapter 5
WILDLIFE

Yellowstone is full of amazing wildlife. The land has a huge amount of diversity. For example, it is home to 67 kinds of mammals. That is more than almost anywhere in the United States. Bison are the park's largest mammal. These creatures roam freely over the land.

Yellowstone National Park has the country's largest bison population on public land.

The park also includes huge predators. Black bears and grizzly bears eat everything they can find. Bobcats and Canada lynx hunt rodents. Wolves are another common predator. Many small animals live in Yellowstone, too. These include yellow-bellied marmots. They are a type of large squirrel. They stay in grassy and rocky areas.

ELK ALL OVER

Elk are common in Yellowstone. They live in many areas across the park. Autumn is mating season for elk. They gather in open areas. Male elk make loud noises called bugles. The elk may even fight.

Male elk have large antlers. They regrow them every year.

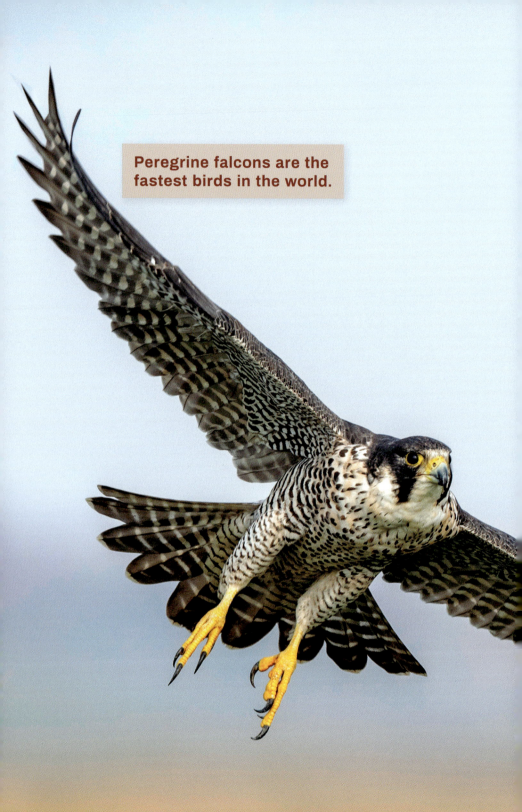

Peregrine falcons are the fastest birds in the world.

Yellowstone's habitats are great for birds. Bald eagles live near water. They hunt for fish. Peregrine falcons live by the sides of cliffs. They watch for smaller birds to hunt. In total, more than 300 bird species live in Yellowstone. Some kinds make nests and raise young in the park. Others stay briefly. Then they fly to other areas.

WATER BIRDS

The trumpeter swan is North America's biggest water bird. Trumpeter swans live in Yellowstone's wetland areas. Loons live in the park's waters, too. Both birds have loud calls.

Cutthroat trout are the state fish of Wyoming, Idaho, and Montana.

Yellowstone has a thriving water ecosystem. Twelve native fish species swim in the park's waters. Cutthroat trout are the most well known. Two kinds of cutthroat live in waters connected to the Yellowstone River. Many non-native fish live in Yellowstone, too.

Columbia spotted frogs are omnivores. They eat plants and insects.

Yellowstone is home to many frogs and salamanders. Columbia spotted frogs are a common type. They are found in areas with lots of plants. Western tiger salamanders live in ponds and lakes. They have bony points on the bottom of their feet.

A SCARY BITE

Several kinds of snakes live in Yellowstone. Most are harmless. But one kind is dangerous. The bite of a rattlesnake can be very painful. It can even lead to death if it is not treated.

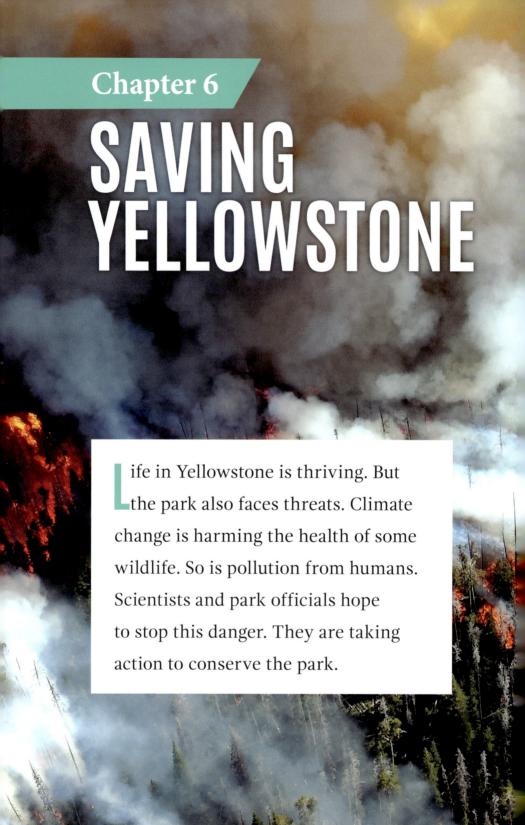

Chapter 6
SAVING YELLOWSTONE

Life in Yellowstone is thriving. But the park also faces threats. Climate change is harming the health of some wildlife. So is pollution from humans. Scientists and park officials hope to stop this danger. They are taking action to conserve the park.

Climate change increases the risk of wildfires.

Some projects focus on wildlife balance. For example, in the 1990s, gray wolves were in danger. Fewer lived in Yellowstone than ever before. The park started a new project. People brought more wolves into Yellowstone. It was a success. By the 2020s, the gray wolf population was stable.

INVASIVE LAKE TROUT

Park workers are trying to stop invasive animals. A project for invasive lake trout began in 1995. Since then, workers have removed more than four million trout from the park's waters.

Gray wolves help the ecosystem by hunting prey.

Golden eagles can have wingspans of more than 7 feet (2.1 m).

Scientists also collect information in the park. For example, some scientists carefully watch Yellowstone's golden eagles. Others collect data about frogs and salamanders. They look for patterns in population growth or decline.

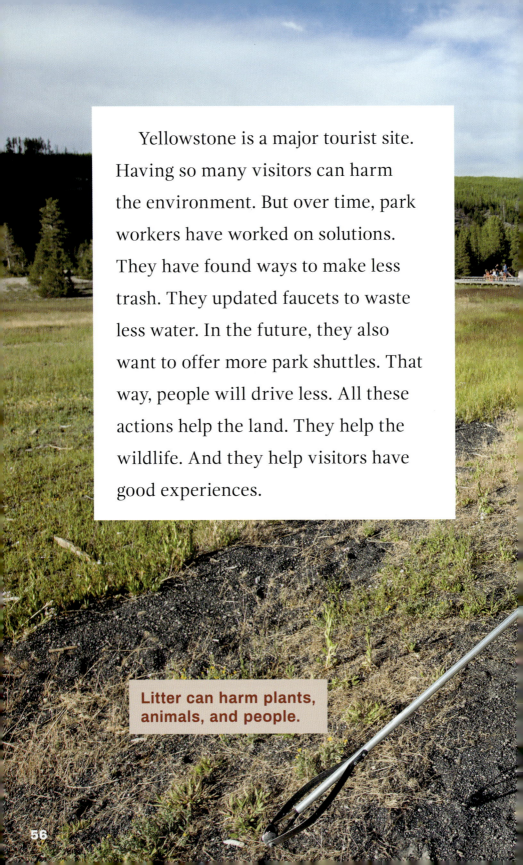

Yellowstone is a major tourist site. Having so many visitors can harm the environment. But over time, park workers have worked on solutions. They have found ways to make less trash. They updated faucets to waste less water. In the future, they also want to offer more park shuttles. That way, people will drive less. All these actions help the land. They help the wildlife. And they help visitors have good experiences.

Litter can harm plants, animals, and people.

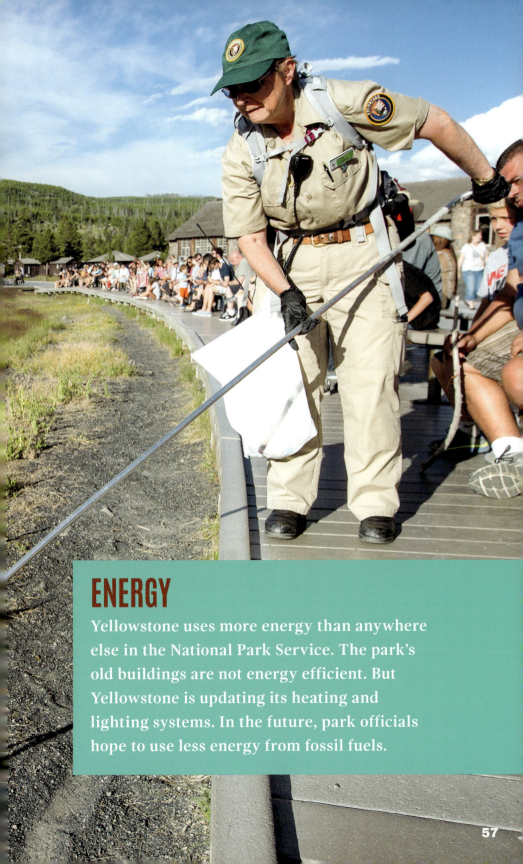

ENERGY

Yellowstone uses more energy than anywhere else in the National Park Service. The park's old buildings are not energy efficient. But Yellowstone is updating its heating and lighting systems. In the future, park officials hope to use less energy from fossil fuels.

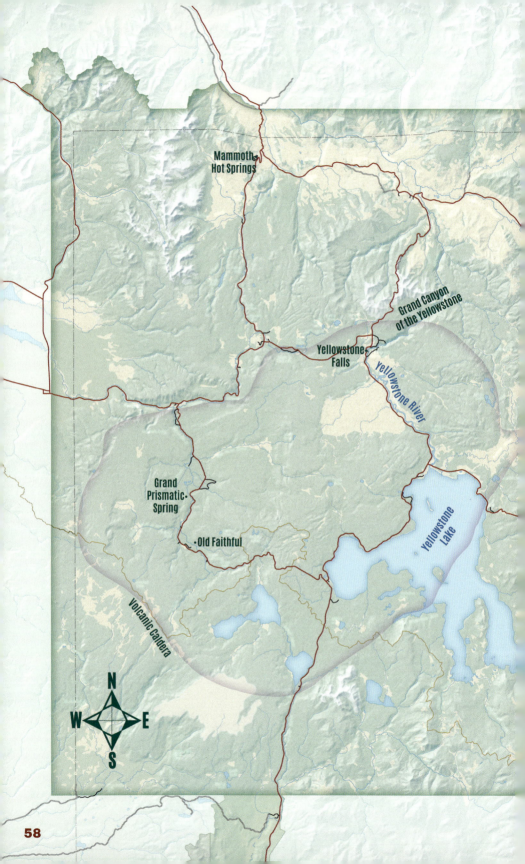

PARK MAP

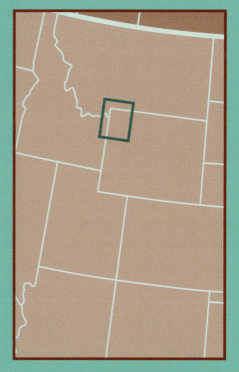

COMPREHENSION QUESTIONS

Write your answers on a separate piece of paper.

1. Write a few sentences explaining the main ideas of Chapter 6.

2. If you visited Yellowstone, what would you be most excited to see? Why?

3. When did the US government make Yellowstone a national park?

   A. 1835
   B. 1872
   C. 1995

4. How could removing invasive animals help native animals survive?

   A. Native animals would die without invasive animals living nearby.
   B. Native animals would not have to compete with invasive animals.
   C. Native animals would move to new places and find better food.

5. What does **thriving** mean in this book?

*Life in Yellowstone is **thriving**. But the park also faces threats. Climate change is harming the health of some wildlife.*

    A. getting louder
    B. having problems
    C. doing well

6. What does **conserve** mean in this book?

*Scientists and park officials hope to stop this danger. They are taking action to **conserve** the park.*

    A. to build more roads in an area
    B. to make something more dangerous
    C. to protect something from harm

Answer key on page 32.

GLOSSARY

climate change
A dangerous long-term change in Earth's temperature and weather patterns.

dormant
Alive but not active, as if in a deep sleep.

energy efficient
When energy is used without much waste.

fossil fuels
Energy sources that come from the remains of plants and animals that died long ago.

fossils
Remains of plants and animals that lived long ago.

Indigenous
Related to the original people who lived in an area.

invasive
Spreading quickly in a new area and causing many problems there.

mating season
The time of year when animals form pairs and come together to have babies.

predictable
When people can guess what will happen in the future.

TO LEARN MORE
BOOKS

Borgert-Spaniol, Megan. *Gray Wolves: Yellowstone's Hunters*. Minneapolis: Abdo Publishing, 2020.

Bowman, Chris. *Yellowstone National Park*. Minneapolis: Bellwether Media, 2023.

Hutchison, Patricia. *Yellowstone's Boiling River*. Minneapolis: Abdo Publishing, 2021.

ONLINE RESOURCES

Visit **www.apexeditions.com** to find links and resources related to this title.

ABOUT THE AUTHOR

Trudy Becker lives in Minneapolis, Minnesota. She likes exploring new places and loves anything involving books. She hopes to visit Yellowstone soon.

INDEX

bears, 42
birds, 45, 55
bison, 18, 25, 40

canyon, 34, 38
Cascade Lake Trail, 34
climate change, 50
conservation, 50, 52, 55–57

elk, 20, 42

fishing, 37
forests, 17, 34
fossils, 17
frogs, 49, 55

geysers, 4, 6, 12, 31–32, 34
Grand Loop, 35
Grand Prismatic Spring, 28, 35

hiking, 34
hot springs, 12–13, 28, 31, 37
hydrothermal features, 11–13, 31

Indigenous peoples, 18, 20, 23

lakes, 14–15, 34, 37, 49

National Park Service, 27, 57
Northern Loop trail, 34

Old Faithful, 4, 6, 32, 35

pollution, 50

salamanders, 49, 55
supervolcano, 11
swimming, 37

thermophiles, 13
trout, 47, 52
Tukudika people, 20

Volcanic Caldera, 11, 31

white settlers, 20, 23, 25
wolves, 42, 52

ANSWER KEY:

1. Answers will vary; 2. Answers will vary; 3. B; 4. B; 5. C; 6. C